D1606276

Southwest Writers Series 35
General Editor: James W. Lee

John Howard Griffin

BY JEFF H. CAMPBELL
Southwestern University

52828

STECK-VAUGHN COMPANY   AUSTIN, TEXAS
An Intext *Publisher*

Jeff H. Campbell is Herman Brown Professor of English and Chairman of the Department of English at Southwestern University. A native of Beaumont, Texas, he was educated at Lamar College, Southern Methodist University, and Duke University, where he was a Gurney Harriss Kearns Fellow and a Dempster Fellow while pursuing studies leading to the doctorate. He was the recipient of the Outstanding Professor Award at Southwestern University in 1964, 1966, and 1970, and has written a number of articles in the fields of American and contemporary literature. He is president of the Texas Association of Departments of English and Vice President of the American Studies Association of Texas. In 1968 he was Visiting Professor at the Perkins School of Theology of Southern Methodist University.

AUTHOR'S ACKNOWLEDGMENT

I should like to thank John Howard Griffin for his graciousness in granting me a personal interview and for making available to me materials which would have been otherwise unobtainable.

John Howard Griffin

John Howard Griffin

John Howard Griffin, whom the literary critic Maxwell Geismar has termed "a Texas Balzac," may be considered a typical Southwest writer only in that he, like most writers of the region, exhibits a rugged and unique individuality. He was born, and once again lives, in Texas, and one of his books is an important contribution to the history of the Texas Staked Plains area; but, educated in France, he frequently writes the first drafts of his novels in French, and the settings for his first two novels are as far from the familiar land of cowboys and Indians as a French Benedictine monastery to the east and an isolated South Pacific island to the west. Although his novels display the earthiness and the scenes of broad sexual comedy and social satire common to more typical Southwestern lore, they are dominated by a philosophical, theological, and mystical sophistication unusual not only in the literature of the Southwest but also in American literature in general. Furthermore, his published work thus far is almost equally divided between highly imaginative artistic works and works of careful sociological reporting. Clearly Griffin combines in himself unusual polarities of gifts and concerns. A brief look at Griffin the man will help clarify the development of these gifts and the origins of these concerns.

Griffin was born in Dallas, June 16, 1920, but grew up in Fort Worth, where he attended public schools until the age of fifteen. At that time, frustrated with the school's inability to challenge his unusually bright mind and his photographic memory, he penned a letter addressed simply to "Headmaster, School for Boys, Tours, France," asking to be allowed to come to Tours to attend school. He wanted Greek, Hebrew, and other courses unavailable in Texas in the mid-thirties, and he volunteered to scrub floors if necessary to earn his tuition at the French school. Weeks later he received a reply saying that if he wanted an education that badly, he was welcome to come—and he would not be required to scrub floors! When presented with this letter of acceptance, the elder Griffins, who had known nothing of the project, were shocked; but they soon realized that they must let their son go.

At the age of fifteen John Griffin went to France to study at the Lycée Descartes in Tours. Upon completion of his work there, he stayed in Tours, enrolling at the École de Medécine, where he pursued medical studies in the mornings and audited courses in French language and literature at the nearby University of Poitiers in the afternoons. As a medical student, Griffin's main interest was in psychiatry, and after his first year of medical studies he began doing extern work under Dr. Pierre Fromenty at the Asylum of Tours. He was engaged in experimental work with the therapeutic possibilities of music, especially the various modalities of the Gregorian chant, when World War II broke out. All medical personnel were immediately mobilized into the French army, and the nineteen-year-old Griffin found himself in charge of the 120 patients in the women's sector of the asylum.

During the next few months Griffin not only ran the asylum but also dressed wounds for soldiers being returned from the front in the middle of the night so that the public would not know the seriousness of the war situation. Furthermore, he participated in

2

smuggling German- and Austrian-Jewish families to the port of St. Nazaire for passage to England. As France's fall became imminent, word of his resistance activities reached the authorities, and he was obliged to leave France in the spring of 1940.

Back in the United States, Griffin enlisted in the U. S. Air Force and was sent to the South Pacific, where he served thirty-nine months. At Dr. Fromenty's suggestion, he carried with him books and texts to continue a serious study of music—harmony, counterpoint, theory—in preparation for continued work in music therapy after the war. He broadcast radio concerts of recorded music to front-area troops and taught composition to combat fatigue cases. A skilled linguist, he volunteered to live among primitive peoples on non-strategic islands in order to learn their languages and cultures, a move calculated to help provide entree for troops if retreat from other islands should prove necessary. He was twice wounded, losing ninety-five percent of his sight as a result of brain damage suffered in a bombing raid near the end of hostilities.

The loss of sight, which he knew would soon become total, forced abandonment of his medical studies, but Griffin returned to France in 1946, determined to utilize his remaining sight in the study of musicology. He specialized in medieval music, particularly the Gregorian chant, and hoped that his studies with Nadia Boulanger, Robert Casadesus, and Jean Batalla might lead to a career as a composer.

When loss of sight became total in 1947, he returned to America to attend schools for the blind and live with his parents on the farm they had purchased at Mansfield, Texas, near Fort Worth. He did extensive lecturing on musicology and devoted himself—quite successfully—to the experimental breeding of livestock in order to show what the blind might accomplish in this field.

In 1949 the critic John Mason Brown was lecturing in the Fort Worth area and came to visit Griffin. After an afternoon's

3

conversation, Brown told Griffin that he should write, that he "talked like a writer." Griffin was astonished at the idea, but the next day he enrolled in a typing course at the Lighthouse for the Blind. He spent two days practicing his typing, and on the third day he began writing his first novel, *The Devil Rides Outside*. He dictated most of the material into a wire recorder, then transcribed it himself, doing much of the first draft in French. In seven weeks the book was finished, and Griffin was confirmed in his vocation as a writer. After several revisions, the book was published in 1952 by Smiths, Inc., of Fort Worth.

Having already discovered that his technical knowledge of the rules of music inhibited his ability to compose (for example, he was so conscious of the necessity to avoid parallel fifths and octaves that he was not free to be creative in musical composition), Griffin decided not to study writing techniques as he took up his literary career. Rather, he sought to transfer what he knew of musical form to the writing of literature. Therefore, he chose Beethoven's C Sharp String Quartet, Op. 131, as a model and sought to build his novel on a similar pattern—"building themes from fragments," as he puts it. He has continued this practice, choosing different musical works as bases for structuring subsequent novels.

In 1952 Griffin, who had been an Episcopalian, became a convert to Catholicism. He felt that he had struggled in *The Devil Rides Outside* to give all the arguments against the Roman Church, and when the book turned out the way it did, he realized that if he did not become a Catholic, he would be living a lie. In 1953 he married the former Elizabeth Ann Holland, a former music student of his whom he had coached for a recital. He pursued his writing despite continuing blindness and other medical difficulties, and his second novel, *Nuni*, written during a period of deep emotional crisis, was published by Houghton Mifflin in association with Smiths in 1956.

4

In 1957, after lengthy medical treatment, his sight was partially restored, and for the first time he was able to see his wife and his two elder children, Susan and John Howard, Jr. His two younger children, Gregory and Amanda, were born in 1958 and 1966.

Undertaking the project of writing a history of the Staked Plains area of Texas, Griffin went to Midland, Texas, in 1958. This project was sponsored by the First National Bank of Midland, which published the resulting book, Land of the High Sky, in 1959.

In November, 1959, under the sponsorship of Sepia magazine, Griffin undertook his famous experiment of darkening his skin and traveled through the Deep South posing as a Negro. The results of this experiment were a series of articles in Sepia and the sensational best seller Black Like Me, first published by Houghton Mifflin in 1961 and made into a movie in 1964. Violent reaction to the book in Mansfield forced the Griffin family to move to Mexico for a while, but growing calls for lectures soon led to their return to the United States and residence in Fort Worth.

Since 1961 Griffin has lectured all across the United States and Canada on various aspects of racism. He has continued to write, publishing numerous articles, short stories, and fragments of works in progress. In 1968 Houghton Mifflin published The John Howard Griffin Reader, edited by Bradford Daniel, which contains condensed versions of Griffin's first four books and extensive selections from other published and unpublished writings of his, including short stories, articles, and selections from both journals and works in progress. The Reader also provides a section of photographs made by Griffin featuring people whose faces had caught and held his interest. These pictures, ranging in subject from lowly Mexican peasants to world-renowned personages such as Thomas Merton and Jacques Maritain, show Griffin to be a gifted and sensitive photographer. In 1969 Pflaum Press published his latest book, The Church and the Black Man. At the time of this writing (early 1970), two more books are scheduled for publication by Houghton Mifflin: *Scattered Shadows*, an autobiography of the years of blindness and sight recovery, and *Street of the Seven Angels*, a novel. Another novel, *Passacaglia*, now in its fifth draft, will have to wait for publication until after the completion of the official biography of Thomas Merton, to which Griffin will devote his entire time and energy through mid-1971.

To date, Griffin has published five major books, in addition to which he has produced a significant body of other work; but an examination of the five major books in the order of their publication seems to be the best way to trace the growth of Griffin's writing talent and his writer's conscience. After analyzing the major works, we can turn more advantageously to smaller, scattered works, describe the nature of work currently in progress, offer a final evaluation of Griffin's present accomplishments, and speculate upon his future achievement.

It is traditional to assume that an author's first novel draws heavily from personal experience and is therefore largely autobiographical. The protagonist of John Howard Griffin's first novel, *The Devil Rides Outside*, is a young American musicologist who is studying priceless medieval manuscripts in the paleography room of a French Benedictine monastery, and certain parallels to Griffin's own career are obvious. He clearly draws on his experiences of intense study in the Benedictine Abbey of Solesmes, his knowledge of Gregorian chant, his familiarity with the French people and countryside, and his own spiritual struggle with the Catholic faith. These obvious autobiographical parallels have led at least one reviewer to state that the book was begun as memoirs and only later converted into a novel. Griffin himself, however, denies this, insisting that the work was an effort of creative imagination from the start, and his statement is supported by the already cited circumstances under which he began the novel at the suggestion of John Mason Brown.

6

Granted the artistic necessity of drawing on one's personal experiences as grist for the creative mill, the imaginative independence of this novel as a true work of art is clear to the careful reader. The deliberate refusal to identify either the protagonist or the exact location of the story contributes to its universality, lifting it above mere autobiography and suggesting that the reader identify with the protagonist and narrator. Clearly, the life being so intimately unfolded is not merely that of a particular individual somewhere in an isolated French monastery. The spiritual struggle here revealed is the struggle of every man, and the use of the first-person journal form and present tense contribute a vivid immediacy.

The title of the book is drawn from an old French proverb which states that "the devil rides outside monastery walls." The proverb provides further evidence of the author's aesthetic distance from his material and supplies a device for adding objectivity and universality to the story. It scts the stage for the central struggle of the protagonist, who finds himself living within the monastery, at first strongly repelled by the rigidity and seeming sterility of the monastic life, but at the same time strangely attracted to its simplicity, peace, and mystical fulfillment. He is drawn to try to understand the devotion and faith of the monks, but the temptations of the outer world are very strong, especially when ill health forces him to move from the monastery to more comfortable quarters in the nearby village. Here he must face the temptations of the Devil—both temptations of the flesh and of the spirit—without the protection of monastery walls.

The proverb also provides the major structural division of the novel. The first part of the book, made up of journal entries from October 12 to December 25, is titled "The Cloister Within," and delineates the hero's growing understanding of monastic life; his concurrent attraction-revulsion to what he sees; his succumbing to the temptation of the flesh in the form of the visiting widow,

Madame Vincent; his bout with recurring malaria, which leads to the necessity of moving from the cold and drafty monastery; and his meeting with a saintly Jesuit and the Rabelaisian Dr. Castelar.

The second half of the book, titled "The Devil Without," begins with the entry for January 1, as the hero moves to a rented villa to be fed and looked after by Madame Renée, a widow and one of the "great ladies" of the village. He returns to the monastery during the day to continue his studies, but afterwards he must face the "devil" who rides outside the monastery in the form of many temptations, primarily Madame Renée herself. She seeks to dominate his life and make of him first a substitute for her two lost sons—one lost in the war and the other to a monastery—and finally a substitute for her dead husband.

The contrast between the asceticism of the monastery and the lustful nature of temptations in the outside world has been noted by most reviewers of the book, and has led some commentators to suggest an undue preoccupation with sex on the part of the author. R. W. Henderson, writing in the *Library Journal* for November, 1952, even suggested that Griffin's "frank treatment of sex outdoes Henry Miller" and commented that interest in the book would likely be limited to specialists in *psychopathia sexualis*. It is true that the book does center around the hero's efforts to come to terms with sexuality and that sexual desires and experiences are described vividly. These descriptions, most notably that of the sexual climax experienced with Madame Vincent (p. 125), led to a censorship controversy. A representative of Pocket Books, which published a 1954 paperback edition of the novel, was arrested in Detroit for selling obscene literature. The Detroit city court convicted the salesman; but after a lengthy series of appeals, the United States Supreme Court heard the case (Butler vs. Michigan) and declared unconstitutional the Michigan penal code forbidding the sale of any publication *containing* obscene, immoral, lewd, or

8

lascivious material. This decision opened the way for more liberal judicial treatment of the obscenity question in which the value of the book as a whole became more important than particular words or isolated scenes. This controversy also aroused Griffin to do research and writing in the field of censorship (see bibliography).

It is somewhat ironic that a book concerned primarily with a spiritual struggle should become a center of controversy over obscenity. Undue concern about the sexual aspects of the book is based on a misreading and misunderstanding of the book's central thesis. Sexual desires and experiences are dealt with vividly and explicitly, but they are dealt with as symbolic of that earthy part of man's nature which comes into conflict with his spiritual aspirations. The monastery stands in stark contrast to the world surrounding it, representing the struggle within every man who is born both as subject to the laws of nature and as peculiarly God's creature, endowed with possibilities of free will, self-realization, and self-giving love. Griffin's thesis is not that the monastery is holy because it denies humanity and sexuality. He makes it quite clear that the monks who have achieved sanctity have not truncated a part of their humanity and achieved an unnatural state thereby. They have recognized and accepted their ordinary human animality, but have chosen to offer this to God. The outside world is potentially not less holy than the monastery. The trouble is that those outside, like Madame Renée, often pretend to a holiness which is hypocritical because they have not honestly faced and accepted who they are. They cripple themselves and heartlessly cripple others because they refuse to recognize their complex natures—sinful beings, yet possessing the possibility for grace— and insist on pouring others into their own warped molds.

For Griffin the term "sanctity" parallels the psychiatric term "adjustment." Sanctity is not achieved by denying the so-called "baser" aspects of man's nature, but by affirming and accepting a

9

wholeness. Salvation for Griffin assumes its original root meaning of health. Sex becomes symbolic, then, of what the Puritan temper would consider base, to be denied or suppressed. For Griffin, however, this "base" side of man is merely the other side of man's double nature which must be affirmed and integrated into a whole that includes the higher aspirations of a St. Augustine, a St. Thomas, or a Gerard Manley Hopkins, whose untitled sonnet No. 69 provides the epigraph for Part I of the book. Griffin has said that one might state the central theme of all his work as "the humanization of man." By this he seems to mean that man must recognize his finite creatureliness, with its natural desires, as being under God, from Whom come the motions of grace which pull the creature beyond himself.

The thesis of the wholeness of man is graphically illustrated in *The Devil Rides Outside* in that the exact words which are used to describe the sexual climax the protagonist experiences with Madame Vincent are also used to describe his mystical experience of union with the Virgin Mary (p. 363). There is no dichotomy between flesh and spirit for the man who has achieved true sanctity. Dr. Castelar, one of the strikingly original characters, seeks to explain this to the protagonist near the end of the first section of the book. The doctor is a passionate and earthy individual, but he is presented as a "truly great Christian" by the saintly Jesuit Marie-Ornoux, a much more typical though still impressive representative of Christian holiness.

At first the protagonist does not comprehend all that Dr. Castelar tells him, but by the end of the novel he has come to understand that faith does not involve an abnegation of self but rather the very opposite—the truest fulfillment of the whole self. He has managed to resist the temptation of simple sensuality represented by the peasant girl Christianne; he has recognized a healthy, nourishing affirmation of sexuality in Mother Nourrie, a simple old woman of the earth-mother type; he has accepted the idea of the holiness and health of marriage presented him by the humanistically intellectual Mademoiselle Marthe; and he has successfully resisted the selfish and prideful temptations of Madame Renée. It is most significant that although sexuality enters into the relationship with Madame Renée, sex here is secondary—only an adjunct to the more central temptation to pride and hypocrisy. The hero has a deep understanding of Madame Renée which tempers and complicates his ambivalent feelings toward her, but he finally resists, without at the same time destroying her.

The novel concludes at Easter time, with its connotations of new birth and resurrection. Madame Renée admits defeat and leaves quietly for England; the hero returns to the monastery, not to reject the outside world, but merely to complete his studies. He concludes his journal with the entry "night of all nativities. Night of all nights with its waking morning." Soon he will leave the monastery to marry and pursue his career, but with a new strength, a new wholeness, a new self-understanding that has removed his fear of the devil who rides outside the monastery walls.

Such a brief discussion can do little more than lift up a few of the many richnesses of such a big book (596 pages), and can only suggest some of the reasons which led Maxwell Geismar to affirm that it stands with James Jones's *From Here to Eternity* and William Styron's *Lie Down in Darkness* as one of the three best novels of the 1950's. Geismar's enthusiasm was not widely shared among critics, and he is almost single-handedly responsible for maintaining interest in this novel through the chapter he devotes to it and to Griffin in his widely read *American Moderns*. The novel is weakened by too much talk, frequently inadequate motivation, and a tendency toward overwriting. But the vivid immediacy of a deeply felt personal experience coupled with clear overtones of an almost allegorical universality, as well as the struggle to understand the meaning of real faith as opposed to false piety or shallow agnosticism, make this a remarkable first novel. As B. R. Redman pointed out in *Saturday Review* (November 1, 1952), the novel throbs with the "power of life," and as *Time* suggested (November 3, 1952), it is striking in that it conveys "some things relatively rare in U. S. letters: energy, earnestness, and unashamed religious fervor."

Energy, earnestness, religious fervor, and the use of the first-person point of view and the present tense provide almost the only direct threads of continuity between *The Devil Rides Outside* and Griffin's second novel, *Nuni*. *Nuni* is set on an isolated island in the South Pacific, totally removed from the ancient culture and civilization of Europe. The protagonist, this time given a name and a fully delineated background, is thrust into a hostile and primitive environment with no protective monastery walls—with no protection, in fact, of any kind—and is forced to fall back on his inner resources. Like the earlier novel, *Nuni* is concerned with a personal and spiritual struggle. The conclusion of this struggle is similar to that implied in *The Devil Rides Outside*, but this time the conclusion is stated much more specifically and cogently.

The protagonist of *Nuni* is John W. Harper, an assistant professor of literature at a small Southern college. He is fifty-seven years old, happily married and the father of three children. He is returning from a reunion with his brother in the Philippines when his plane crashes and he finds himself the sole survivor, washed up on the shore of an uninhabited Pacific reef. Griffin conceived the idea for the novel as he thought about his own experiences during his army assignments in World War II living among isolated island people untouched by civilization. He began to speculate: "What would happen to the average American of this day and age if he were suddenly stripped of all the paraphernalia of his life and thrust among total primitives?" Griffin had kept careful and complete notes on his observations, especially of an island the natives called "Nuni." "Nuni" meant, in their language, "world," and this small island was indeed the whole world to them (and, because of their ignorance, the only world they had any desire to know). Drawing on his records of the actual culture on the island of Nuni, Griffin recreates with anthropological exactness the rituals, customs, and taboos of a primitive people and examines their effect upon Professor Harper, who represents "the average American of this day and age."

The book opens with Professor Harper on the plane that will carry him to his wife and family. He observes his fellow passengers and comments especially on the "acid goodness" of a young missionary across the aisle. He thinks of home and imagines the scenes of his homecoming, thus introducing the stream-of-consciousness technique that dominates the first portion of the novel. The explosion that destroys the plane ends chapter one, and chapter two opens as Harper finds himself in the ocean, struggling through the breakers to a beach in a cove surrounded by cliffs.

The balance of Book I conveys Harper's struggles with hunger and thirst, with the searing heat of the day and the chilling nights, and with his bewildering efforts to explore the reef around him. The visual images communicate a vivid immediacy, especially striking when one realizes that they were written by a man six years without sight. By strenuously visualizing details in his mind, Griffin sought to describe the sea, the reef, the sun, and the night so that no reader would guess his lack of sight.

The visual sharpness of detail contrasts significantly with Harper's growing inability to distinguish between one moment and the next, between past and present, between mirage and reality. The stream-of-consciousness technique effectively introduces the reader to the personality that is John Harper and draws him into the experience that leads Harper to struggle to define himself anew,

13

cut off as he is from all the experiences that defined him previously. Harper explores his island, and on several occasions he thinks he sees smoke or hears a cock crow or views the shadowy shapes of men on a distant beach. He cannot find the source of the smoke or a settlement with chickens, however; and when he returns to the spot on the beach where he thought he saw human figures, he realizes that the footprints he finds are his own. He recalls incidents from his past, but significantly is unable to remember his wife's face. Separated as he is from all that he was, he cannot bring into sharp outline the face of the person who had meant the most to him.

After an indeterminate number of days of such existence, Harper awakes one morning to find that he has been discovered by a small black boy. The boy feeds him coconut, and returns the next day with an old man. Afterwards, the two come daily, supplying Harper with food and drink. Slowly they teach him the native language, but they make no move to bring him to their village. Although they are providing him subsistence, he is struck by their utter lack of feeling for him or for each other. He is as keenly aware as ever of his human isolation. Harper comments: "Strange how savages could do this to a supposedly educated man; strange how all the education of the civilized world cannot counter the simple growth of emotions, cannot nullify the feelings of death when respect and affection are denied you" (p. 109).

Book II opens as the boy comes to take Harper to the village to celebrate the death of a man named Maigna and to live in Maigna's now-vacant hut. He is shocked to learn that for these people death is the ultimate good of a dark, predestined, painful life. Rauka, the sorceress, says at the burial, "We leave you in sunlight, and we go back and wait in the shadow" (p. 160). Harper also finds that sex is considered evil. A man marries out of duty to perpetuate the race, but he considers each sexual act a diminishing of his man-

14

hood. Mating is an unpleasant duty to be endured, not a joy to be celebrated. Furthermore, the native language has no words for intimate parts of the body; they are taboo, and all acts of urination or defecation must be performed hidden from sight in the depths of the jungle. If anyone sees another performing such an act, he gains possession of the other's spirit.

There is no emotion, compassion, or joy among the people, and their lives are made bearable only by their daily chewing of narcotic betel nuts. Children are not even given names at birth. This curious inattention has a practical basis: so many of the children die as the result of the ritual tattooing at age four or five that it is deemed needless effort to give them names until one is sure that they will survive.

Harper finds the only hints of joy or affection to be among the small children who have not yet been tattooed, who have not yet been conditioned to accept the dark life of the tribe. When a small and as yet nameless girl approaches him one day, he plays with her as he might with any child at home, and since she is so small he gives her a name—Ririkinger, which means finger. A club brought sharply to the back of his head lets him know that to touch a female, even a small nameless one, is taboo. Even this small expression of natural love and joy is not tolerated.

When the time arrives for the girl whom he has named Ririkinger to be tattooed by the sorceress, Harper intervenes and trades the elder a gold locket with pictures of his own children in order to obtain possession of the girl and thus protect her from the cruel cutting and danger of death. By sacrificing the only link he has with all that has been dear to him in the past for the innocent life of another, Harper recovers a sense of his own humanity. Rauka will not give up her victim without a fight, but Harper defeats her and rescues Ririkinger for a life without tattoos. She is thus spared the physical scars of human bondage to superstition, and the hope

15

is that she will also be spared the psychic and spiritual scars and be freed for a truly human life.

Despite flashbacks and reflections introduced by the stream-of-consciousness device, the plot line moves forward clearly, simply, and compellingly, developing the central theme of the harshness and darkness to which man so easily becomes enslaved without a recognition of love, compassion, and free will. If Griffin has followed his usual method of structuring his books on musical patterns, the structure here is the simpler pattern of a single theme with variations rather than a more complex pattern such as the sonata form. As Harper reflects on what he has done and what he has become, however, Griffin takes his single theme and swells it into a fugue to clarify the meaning of Harper's story.

Harper finds himself haunted by the phrase "driven along paths not of their own choosing." This phrase becomes the "fugal theme to the soul's infinite variations" (p. 292), and Harper realizes that the people of Nuni have become enslaved to Elemental Nature, "each soul deadened until there is no living from within, but only from without" (p. 292). The theme resounds in Harper's mind "in a startlingly different key" (p. 297) as he realizes that it is "equally the theme of me and of the people of my world, different only in its counterpoint, in its treatment and its preoccupations" (p. 297). Modern man, he realizes, has allowed himself to become enslaved to Mechanized Nature, which has "contrived to make him forget the forever-hungering goals of his spiritual being" (p. 299). He sees that a freely given love is the only answer to human bondage, and the blazing word love becomes the "majestic coda to the theme, changing it from a minor tonality into that mysterious modality which is neither major nor minor, but multi-hued in strengths, and tones and softnesses..." (p. 301).

The climax is a little heavy, a little too explicit for sophisticated modern tastes suspicious of all hints of didacticism; the fugal gran-

16

deur is a bit rich to emerge from the simplicity of the theme from which it grows. But Harper's story has been so realistically and convincingly told, the people of Nuni so believably re-created, and the implications for modern life so powerfully stated that one cannot forget this memorable fugue of faith and love or wish it left unstated. Harper has discovered the key to the full humanization of man, and although he still has no prospects for leaving the island, the suggestion is clear that the island itself may change through his influence. As the book closes, already "the atmosphere is new, freed of the taint of evil, freed of constraint and fear" (p. 310).

In many ways *Nuni* is a better novel than *The Devil Rides Outside*. It is half as long, and thus free of some of the excesses of the earlier novel. Its simple, compelling plot line is easier to follow than the Beethovian complexities of fragmented themes in *The Devil Rides Outside*. Its conclusion, emphasizing the wholeness of man—"the goodness of both his angel-demands and his animal-demands" (p. 300)—echoes the ending of the earlier novel, but it bases its point on a simpler story and avoids the complications of mysticism and sex. *Nuni* will probably remind the student of contemporary literature of William Golding's more famous *Lord of the Flies*, with its similar treatment of primitive savagery. Although the conclusion of Griffin's book may incline one to consider it, like Golding's, a fable, with incidents carefully chosen to support a controlling thesis and lead to a predetermined climax, the anthropological details of *Nuni* are more exact and more convincing than those of *Lord of the Flies*. Its conclusion, though perhaps even more specific in its message than Golding's, also grows more naturally out of the story told and seems therefore less contrived. *Nuni* deserves a much wider reading than it has so far received.

John Howard Griffin's third book, *Land of the High Sky*, occupies an important and unique position in the Griffin canon, but is probably the least well known of all his works. It is a relatively brief (180 pages of text) but vividly colorful history of the area centering around Midland, Texas, from its first exploration by Captain Randolph Marcy in 1849 through its development as a metropolitan oil and ranching center by 1959. The book was Griffin's first major project after recovering his sight; it was his initial nonfiction work; and it is his only work thus far dealing with traditional Southwestern regional material. Highly and justly praised, the book's vivid and sympathetic re-creation of the life of the cowboy on the plains has been likened to the work of J. Frank Dobie, whom Griffin knew and admired. The entire narrative conveys a liveliness and believability uncommon and unexpected in such historical studies.

Although it is required reading in many college courses in Western Americana, the book remains largely unknown because it was published in a limited edition by the First National Bank in Midland to celebrate the opening of its new building, which coincided with the centennial of Marcy's exploration of the area. Bradford Daniel has included the "Preface" and two chapters (chapter 1, "Eighteen Covered Wagons," and chapter 7, "Cowboy") in his *John Howard Griffin Reader*. Daniel also includes a highly amusing section called "The Love Letters of Bessie Love" which had to be omitted from the original edition of *Land of the High Sky* because of space limitations. This section, a welcome addition to the annals of frontier humor, tells the hilarious story of a hoax a group of cowboys pulled on an unfortunate advertiser in the *Do Not Be a Lonely Heart Register*. In addition, Betsy Feagin Colquitt has chosen to open her *A Part of Space: Ten Texas Writers* with a reprint of "Eighteen Covered Wagons," so at least some of Griffin's contribution to Southwestern lore is becoming more widely available.

The "Preface" to *Land of the High Sky* not only provides a deeply meaningful introduction to the book, but also renders an invalu-

18

able introduction to Griffin and his approach to the task of writing. In it Griffin describes beginning his research by having himself deposited near an isolated water hole on the Foy Proctor ranch. He wanted to experience the land as nearly as possible the way the first settlers had experienced it in the 1880's. As he spent the night alone in the immense silence, he felt he came to understand the land: "Like the desert or the ocean, it throws a man face to face with nature stripped of all distracting elements—no mountains, no trees, no beautiful views, though its very simplicity is more than beauty. It overwhelms. To stay here, a man must face himself and the realities of life and death" (p. vii). "I could understand," he continued, "the early-day rancher's love for it and the cowboy's, as I could understand another's hatred of it" (p. vii).

Griffin's next research led him to newspaper files, court records, and birth, marriage, medical, church, and death records. He began to feel that he knew these long-dead people better in some ways than their contemporaries had, for he learned what foods they ate, what recipes they used, what books they read, how they did the laundry, and even what items were stocked in the drugstore where they shopped.

Finally, after a complete immersion in the land itself, in documents and records of all sorts, and with the people still living and working in the area, Griffin began to write down everything he had gathered. The first manuscript came to 1300 pages. Obviously, some organizing viewpoint was necessary to focus the required cutting-down. Drawing on Virgil's words, "Nature first gave those customs," Griffin decided to center the book around "the land and the peoples who successively lived on it and were formed by it: from the prehistoric man to the modern oil man and industrialist" (p. x).

This pattern then determined the order of the twelve chapters of the book, beginning with the explorations of Captain Marcy and including the dramatic story of the murder by Indians of the young, idealistic Lieutenant M. P. Harrison, grandson of William Henry Harrison (ninth president of the United States) and younger brother of Benjamin Harrison, who became president in 1888. The following chapter graphically details the life of the Comanche Indians, who continued to dominate the Staked Plains area until the early 1880's. Subsequent chapters bring to life the strength, courage, tenacity, and hardships of the early frontiersmen—buffalo hunters, farmers, sheep-raisers, and cattlemen. Chapter six, "Windmill Town," chronicles the early days of Midland itself, crediting, as the title suggests, to the introduction of the windmill the survival of both the town and the surrounding ranches in this arid land of frequent drought.

Chapter seven delineates the life of the plains cowboy, an existence bearing almost no similarity to the familiar cinema version, being one of deep commitment, hard work, and rugged virtue. Chapters eight and nine describe the slow, steady cultural and economic growth of the Midland area, while chapters ten, eleven, and twelve convey the excitement of the oil boom during the 1920's and 1930's and the continuing concurrent growth of both oil and ranching activities. Chapter ten describes the famous "blowing in" of Santa Rita No. 1, the first of the oil wells on the vast and previously-considered-almost-worthless lands of The University of Texas. Griffin also explodes the myth that the location of Santa Rita No. 1 was chosen accidentally because excessive rain caused the equipment to bog down and made drilling necessary at that spot. There was no rain in January, 1921, and the well was spudded down at the exact spot that had been chosen.

Land of the High Sky is a significant contribution to the recording and preserving of part of Texas and Western history. Its colorful, vivid style brings alive the activities, the emotions, the hardships, the strengths and weaknesses of the men and women who pioneered the Staked Plains. Its careful documentation and extensive bibliography provide a mine of information for scholars. And its recipes for son-of-a-gun stew and sourdough bread enable the modern sophisticated reader not only to imagine what life was like on the plains in earlier days, but actually to recreate its taste.

1959 was a fateful year for John Howard Griffin. He was now accustomed to the miracle of restored sight, and his three books had received generally favorable, if limited, critical attention. Nevertheless, Hawthorne's reference to himself as "the obscurest man of letters in America" in 1850 was equally descriptive of Griffin's position more than a hundred years later. As publication of *The Scarlet Letter* altered Hawthorne's situation and brought him national attention and notoriety, so did Griffin's unique experiment of darkening his skin and passing as a Negro in the Deep South. The resultant publication of his experiences, first in *Sepia* magazine and then in *Black Like Me*, launched Griffin into the arena of public attention.

Just as the generally retiring Hawthorne had not set out to produce his novel of adultery as a calculated attempt to bring attention to himself, neither did the gentle, sensitive, and deeply committed Griffin hit upon his experiment as the journalistic trick of a free-lance writer in search of a sensational story. As Hawthorne's novel grew from his dedication to his craft and his fascination with the dark themes of sin and guilt, so Griffin's decision to explore firsthand the effects of racism grew from his long-standing concern with the "humanization of man" and his realization that hatred, rejection, and discrimination are double killers: they dehumanize both the oppressed and the oppressor.

In 1957 Griffin had been doing research on the growing rate of Negro suicide in the South. He found that many Negroes refused to answer his questionnaires, fearing that their answers might be used against them or reprisals taken on their families. Repeatedly he was told: "The only way you can *know* what it is like is to wake up in my skin." Having seen the destructive results of racism in the Nazi persecution of the Jews, and recognizing frightening similarities in many American references to "the Negro problem," Griffin determined to do what he could to take on another's skin by means of sun-lamp treatments and a newly discovered drug. Thus he could travel through the Deep South as a Negro. He determined to change nothing about himself except his skin pigment. He would maintain his name, his speech patterns, his papers, his abilities. If racism were not involved, then he would still be treated as the same man and enjoy the same opportunities. If, on the other hand, racism were involved, then he would find himself judged by pigment alone, and his life as a Negro would be radically different from his life as a white. In any event, he hoped his experience would enable him really to understand the life of a member of a scorned minority, a "second-class citizen."

Although Griffin's family concurred in his plans, they were naturally apprehensive about the effects of his experiment, as was Griffin himself. Griffin was convinced, however, through his extensive theological studies, that the only hope for man lies in his efforts to bring society into conformity with the rule of love and justice, and he turned to the following passage from Jacques Maritain's *Scholasticism and Politics* for courage to pursue his task:

> The general paganization of civilization has resulted in man's placing his hope in force alone and in the efficacy of hate, whereas in the eyes of an integral humanism, a political ideal of brotherly love alone can direct the work of authentic social regeneration; and it follows that to prepare a new age of the world, martyrs to the love of neighbour may first be necessary. . . .

Willing to become a martyr to the love of neighbor, Griffin set out for New Orleans in early November to begin the experiment that was to bring him fame and notoriety, abuse and praise, and determine the course of his life and career for the next ten years.

In New Orleans Griffin contacted a prominent dermatologist who agreed to cooperate in the project. He would attempt to darken Griffin's skin with a medication taken by mouth, followed by treatment with a sun-lamp (ultraviolet rays). The newly discovered drug was used on victims of vitiligo, a disease causing the appearance of white spots on the face and body. The drug could be dangerous, and it usually took from six weeks to three months to accomplish the desired darkening. Griffin felt he could not spare that much time, so it was decided to try to accelerate the treatments, with constant blood tests to ascertain how his system was tolerating the medicine. The treatments were begun on November 2, 1959. Five days later, although the treatment had not worked as completely as Griffin and the doctor had hoped, there was a dark undercoating of pigment which could be touched up easily with stain. The dosage of the medicine was established, and the darkness would increase as time went on. Griffin shaved his straight hair, ground stain into his exposed skin, and prepared to leave the home where he had been staying to begin his life as a Negro.

As he looked into the mirror before leaving, Griffin realized that his transformation was total and shocking.

> In the flood of light against white tile, the face and shoulders of a stranger—a fierce, bald, very dark Negro—glared at me from the glass. He in no way resembled me .... I had expected to see myself disguised, but this was something else .... All traces of the John Griffin I had been were wiped from existence (*Black Like Me*, New American Library edition, p. 15).

Griffin's first experience as a black man confirmed his initial impression. Not only did he feel himself to be a different man; everyone he met treated him as a different man. The white girl in the drugstore he had patronized regularly for the past week showed no hint of recognition. On the bus he sought to indicate with a friendly look that a standing white woman was welcome to take the empty seat beside him—but her only response was a sharp "What are you looking at me like *that* for?" and the loud comment "They're getting sassier every day." He walked to the same shoeshine stand he had been visiting as a white man. Sterling Williams, the Negro operator of the stand, greeted him as a stranger in town, never guessing that this was the same man whose shoes he had shined for nearly a week—even though he did recognize the shoes as being just like those of a white man named Griffin.

Griffin took Williams into his confidence, explaining his experiment and asking to be allowed to work at the stand with him for a while. Williams also helped him learn the necessity for careful planning, since rest rooms and water fountains available to Negroes were few and far between. Griffin soon came to recognize two types of white customers at the shoeshine stand. One type treated the Negro shine boys as machines that had no human existence whatever—"They looked and saw nothing" (p. 30). The other type talked freely, wanting Griffin and Williams to find Negro girls for them. Griffin was disgusted by the patent attitude of these men who conceived Negroes to be of such low morality that nothing could offend them, but, even so, he found them less offensive than the other type, who looked at him as if he were a stone or a post.

Griffin stayed in New Orleans a week, mingling with various strata of Negro society and meeting constant rejection in his attempts to find a job as a typist or bookkeeper. With two exceptions (he was once pursued by a group of white youths and once insulted and humiliated by a bus driver) his contacts with whites were amicable enough, but doors were kept firmly closed. On the other hand, he found Negroes helpful and concerned, especially a young Dillard University student who walked with him over two miles to show him the way to a Negro movie house. At the end of the week Griffin felt that he was achieving growing insight into what it means to be a Negro:

> My first vague, favorable impression that it was not as bad as I had thought it would be came from courtesies of the whites toward the Negro in New Orleans. But this was superficial. All the courtesies in the world do not cover up the one vital and massive discourtesy—that the Negro is treated not even as a second-class citizen, but as a tenth-class one. His day-to-day living is a reminder of his inferior status (p. 47).

He decided to leave New Orleans for a bus trip to Hattiesburg, Mississippi. This bus trip—with its unspoken fear on the part of the Negroes in the back of the bus, its "hate stares" from the whites in the front, and its driver who refused to allow the Negroes off the bus for the scheduled rest stop between New Orleans and Hattiesburg—provides one of the most vivid and poignant passages in *Black Like Me*. In his room upstairs in an unpainted wooden shanty structure in Hattiesburg that night, Griffin realized fully the truth of "Lionel Trilling's remark that culture—learned behavior patterns so deeply engrained they produce unconscious, involuntary reactions—is a prison" (p. 68). Griffin saw the prison his white culture had locked him in, and he was now experiencing the prison of black culture. His experiment was to be an integral step in his continuing efforts to break down the walls of all such cultural prisons, to promote the kind of understanding prerequisite to his desire to contribute to the "humanization of man."

In Hattiesburg Griffin visited with P. D. East, editor of the *Petal Paper*, who had suffered ostracism and reprisals for his espousal of racial justice. East took Griffin back to New Orleans, where he visited briefly at Dillard University and then once more took the bus—this time to Biloxi, Mississippi. From there he hitchhiked to Mobile, Alabama, finding that all but two of the white men who gave him rides picked him up "the way they would pick up a pornographic photograph or book" (p. 85). They showed morbid curiosity about the sex life of the Negro, assuming that the Negro was "an inexhaustible sex-machine with oversized genitals and a vast store of experiences, immensely varied" (p. 85). In Mobile Griffin found the familiar pattern of New Orleans repeated: he was unable to find a job. One plant foreman told him frankly: "No use trying here. . . . We're gradually getting you people weeded out from the better jobs at this plant. We're taking it slow, but we're doing it. Pretty soon we'll have it so the only jobs you can get here are the ones no white man would have" (p. 98).

Hitchhiking from Mobile toward Montgomery, Griffin was picked up by a respectable, respected, white family man and civic leader who told Griffin that he insisted on sexual intercourse with every Negro girl he hired either for housework or in his business. "We figure we're doing you people a favor to get some white blood in your kids," he said (p. 100). Griffin's next ride was from a young Negro man who offered him sleeping space in his two-room cabin, although it was crowded with six children. Despite their poverty, this Negro family displayed a dignity and nobility of spirit that is perhaps as moving to the reader in Griffin's description of it as the experience was to Griffin himself.

Griffin took a bus on to Montgomery, where he found that lack of exposure to the sun had so lightened his skin that he could now "pass for white" by scrubbing off the stain from his face and hands. By re-applying the stain, he could once more "pass" as a Negro. He found that this simple change in color of his skin completely changed his status in the city. As a white, he could go into a fine restaurant and be served with great courtesy. The next day, as a

26

Negro, he was barred from any such possibility. There could be no doubt about racism now. "I was the same man, whether white or black," he wrote. "Yet when I was white, I received the brotherly-love smiles and the privileges from whites and the hate stares or obsequiousness from the Negroes. And when I was a Negro, the whites judged me fit for the junk heap, while the Negroes treated me with great warmth" (pp. 121-22).

A brief visit to Tuskegee Institute at Tuskegee, Alabama, and a bus trip to Atlanta concluded Griffin's cross-country trip as a Negro. In Atlanta he resumed his white identity, did some investigative work for *Sepia* magazine, and then returned to New Orleans to resume his Negro identity long enough to visit his former haunts and be photographed in them.

On December 15, six weeks after starting for New Orleans, he returned home to Mansfield. As news of the experiment became known through television interviews and publication of the installments of "Journey Into Shame" in *Sepia* magazine (April through September, 1960), the expected threats and reprisals materialized. Griffin was burned in effigy on the main street of Mansfield, and he and his parents received numerous threatening, obscene telephone calls. Griffin was forced to hide in the home of friends in Dallas for a few days, but soon decided to return openly to Mansfield and face whatever danger there might be. By August he and his wife decided it was too great an injustice to their children to remain in Mansfield, and they decided to move to Mexico. Griffin had been told that he would be castrated on July 15, but then the date was moved to August 15. He stayed on past that date, determined not to allow the bullies to claim they had "chased him out," but by August 17 the Griffins were packed and headed for Mexico.

By June 19 Griffin had received 6,000 letters—all unsolicited and only nine of them abusive—from various places in the South. This

27

confirmed his contention that the average Southern white was more kindly disposed than he dared allow his neighbor to see, fearing his fellow white racist more than he feared the Negro. Growing recognition of the significance of Griffin's work led to numerous calls to lecture in various parts of the country. The acceptance of such calls made a return to residency in the United States advisable, and the Griffin family returned to Ft. Worth, where they still live.

Black Like Me, the complete record of the skin-darkening experiment, was published by Houghton Mifflin in 1961 and immediately became a best-seller. It was issued as a paperback by the New American Library in 1962 and is currently still selling well in its thirty-ninth printing. In addition, it has been published in England and translated into French, German, Italian, Norwegian, Dutch, Portuguese, Polish, Yugoslav, Hungarian, Czechoslovakian, and Japanese. On the basis of the book and his other work in the area of racism, Griffin has been awarded the *Saturday Review* Anisfield-Wolf Award, the National Council of Negro Women's Award, the Christian Culture Series Award, and the second *Pacem in Terris* Award (the first recipient was the late John F. Kennedy). The movie version of *Black Like Me,* starring the actor James Whitmore, was released in 1964.

Black Like Me, widely read and reviewed, received almost universal acclaim. The straightforward, simple, personal style of narration was an excellent complement to the highly charged emotional impact of the content of the story itself. S. H. Loory, writing in the *New York Herald Tribune* (October 15, 1961), was almost alone in finding the reporting "uneven, at times ungrammatical." Loory's chief criticism was of Griffin's basic premise that "a white man must live a Negro's life to understand his problems." Loory felt that this premise disregarded the white man's capacity to "see through the evils of oppression and discrimination," but he praised Griffin's vivid firsthand accounts of his

28

experiences. The general critical appraisal echoed that of L. E. Lomax, who wrote in *Saturday Review* (December 9, 1961): "*Black Like Me* is a troubling book written by an accomplished novelist. Though slender, this volume is a scathing indictment of our society."

Though admittedly slender in size, and although its author undertook the experiment as a project he thought would be of interest primarily to sociologists, *Black Like Me* launched Griffin into a career of lecturing and further investigations into racism and bigotry that not only brought him national attention but also radically altered the course of his life and career. He had thought this experiment would be a minor sidelight to his central career as a novelist, but the invitations to lecture to sociology classes, psychology classes, law schools, management groups, etc., coupled with his feeling that he now had a competence in the field that must be shared with others, drew him out of his study, away from his projected novels, and into the heat of the Civil Rights controversy of the 1960's.

Griffin continued to work on projects that he considered more in the mainstream of his ongoing vocation as a creative writer, but the bibliography of his published works during the 1960's clearly indicates his involvement with the continuing impact of his concern with bigotry. Of the twenty-nine articles and essays he published during the period, twenty-one deal directly with some aspect of racism. This decade of work was culminated in November, 1969, with the publication of Griffin's fifth major book, *The Church and the Black Man*.

The Church and the Black Man is a strikingly designed book, illustrated with powerful photographs, many of them taken by Griffin himself. These illustrations and the recorded voices of Rev. James Groppi of the Milwaukee NAACP and Rev. Albert Cleage, author of *The Black Messiah* (bound into the volume on a flexible disc), give the book a dramatic impact. Griffin, described on the book jacket as "the foremost interpreter of the black American in a white society," summarizes in his text the insights of his ten years of opposing racism and bigotry, delineates the failures of white churches, seeks to explain the mood of black America, and challenges the church to an eleventh-hour effort to rid itself of racism.

The idea that culture is a prison unless people know the key to unlock the door, central to *Black Like Me* and much of Griffin's other writing and lectures of the 1960's, becomes the unifying thesis of the book. The imprisoning culture expresses itself in a silent language "by which men unknowingly express, through attitudes, springing from learned behavior patterns, truths that contradict their actual words, and of which they may be wholly unconscious" (p. 5). It is this silent language that contributes to a basic duality of viewpoint between white and black. Many white men who honestly believe that they are free of prejudice still operate on the unconscious assumption that blacks are "underdeveloped versions of whites and must be helped to rise up to 'our level' " (p. 6). Such an attitude is degrading to black men and alienates them in a way that is fatal to genuine dialogue. White men, Griffin points out, too often "talk with a black man as though he were a combination of Rap Brown, Uncle Tom, Black Panther, Baptist Preacher, Uncle Ben, and Aunt Jemima rolled into one 'culturally disadvantaged' package ..." (p. 7). The white cultural prison is tragically dehumanizing to the racist himself because he espouses a twisted view of man in which he sees members of other races as "intrinsically other."

The concept of the Negro as the "intrinsic other" had first been systematically explored by Griffin in an essay included in Father Georges Dominique Pire's *Building Peace* in 1966. Here it is lifted up as one of the central elements of the white cultural prison that must be recognized and conquered if the true dialogue that

30

humanizes men of all races is to overcome the duality of viewpoint that divides white and black.

As Griffin sees the situation, the organized church is deeply implicated in the promotion of white racism. "The white church," he says, "without desiring it or intending it, is part of the white society that imposes the system" (p. 25). The black man finds no comfort or help in the splendid statements he reads signed by church leaders, for "he discovers too often that if priests seek to implement such statements, the same bishops who signed the statements suppress the priests" (p. 7).

Griffin indicts all American churches for being guilty of condoning racism, but, as a devout Catholic, he draws most of his illustrations of churchly shortcomings from the Roman Catholic Church. He lists instances of black priests' being ignored, ostracized, or suppressed; he describes *de facto* segregation in Catholic churches "officially" open to all; and he vividly depicts the feeling of betrayal on the part of black Catholics (and many whites, as well) when Judge Leander Perez, an active white racist who had actually been excommunicated for his racist views, was buried with full church honors in a chapel on the campus of Loyola University in New Orleans. Griffin's outspoken criticism of the Church aroused opposition among some of the Catholic hierarchy, but his uncompromising stand resulted in his being invited, with several black priests, to the Vatican in 1969 to describe the situation directly to the Pope himself.

The failure of the churches to make good in practice the glowing statements they officially promulgate is one of the factors Griffin points to as explaining the mood of black America as the Sixties end. The failure of the churches and of white culture in general to be moved by the monumental attempts of Negroes to change their situation by nonviolent resistance is another important factor. For ten years black Americans responded with heroic

31

charity in an effort to "love their oppressors until those oppressors were cured of the terrible sickness of racism, healed and liberated from the need to oppress others" (p. 53). But the nonviolent movement could not succeed unless it converted the hostile force, and white men generally did not show any significant change in attitudes. Griffin personally feels that the nonviolent movement did make many profound changes, but that they were not numerous enough or deep enough to break down the walls of the cultural prison.

The killing of Martin Luther King is seen to be a final positive indication to black men that the dream of an integrated society was an impossible dream, one that weakened black men. White society apparently will continue to look upon the Negro as "intrinsically other" and insist that the black man, if he is to be integrated into white culture, conform to white, middle-class cultural values— in fact, become an imitation white. This would mean detaching himself from his black origins, "wearing a white man's mask," fragmenting himself from his own community, acting as the white man thinks he should. The failure of nonviolent resistance to bring the hoped-for results led many black men to decide that no matter what they did to try to "act white," it would never be enough; they would still be black and looked upon as "intrinsically other."

The alternative for many blacks, then, has been a conscious effort to overcome fragmented individualism by deliberately emphasizing negritude, by turning "black" into a word of pride and beauty, by refusing to wear the "white man's mask" (pp. 82-83). Thus the source of "Black Power" lies in the failure of the dream of an integrated society. "If the dream of an integrated society had been fulfilled," Griffin writes, "then Black Power would be useless and indeed could not exist" (p. 83).

Griffin admits that he regrets "deeply, as do many men, white and black, that attitudes have finally driven black men to abandon many of the old dreams we shared, dreams that were good; and to embark into this period of transition that so bewilders men ..." (p. 70). But he sees positive possibilities in the Black Power movement and thinks that some signs of hope are now present. Black Power does not necessarily imply the advocacy of violence; in fact, it may provide a meaningful alternative to fruitless violent confrontation by turning "the burning resentments and the energies they engendered into healthful and constructive channels" (p. 83).

Although admitting that "the signs are not very encouraging" (p. 98), Griffin believes that it is not too late for white American churches to make a significant contribution to breaking down the walls of the cultural prison separating black and white and threatening to destroy the American dream. The churches must cease implying "that the white man has something to concede to the black man," and must "learn to stop trying to turn black men into merely white Christians" (p. 98). The church needs to "help us see that our differences do not make us enemies. The differences could be an enormous enrichment if the racist Christian would ever stop running long enough to give them a chance to enrich, to humanize, to cure" (p. 98). This kind of cure is needed by all—white men, black men, and the church itself.

Moving from Griffin's five major books to shorter, scattered pieces of writing, we find that the variety of concerns reflected in the books is also present in the other published work. Griffin's small body of short stories published in the Fifties indicates his commitment to the craft of fiction. He himself is not very enthusiastic about the stories, and they certainly do not achieve the complexity and impact of his novels, but, like the novels, they reflect his concern for the "humanization of man," and are told with skill and frequent high humor.

Perhaps the best of the short stories is "Sauce for the Gander," first published in 1953 in *New World Writing 3* and then reprinted in the widely used anthology *Communicative Reading*, edited by Otis J. Aggertt and Elbert R. Brown. The story describes the quandary of a simple old monk who tends the geese in the Abbey of Dleifsnam. One of his geese has hurt her leg, and he must keep her caged and bandaged in order for the leg to heal. She is downcast and will not eat, however, because her gander has taken up with a much younger goose—and after only three days, too! The simple monk is genuinely worried about what he should do, and seeks the counsel of the abbot on a "question of morals." The abbot and the other monks dismiss the whole affair, insisting that animals should not be expected to have the morals of humans. The simple solution seems to be to kill the goose and serve her to the monks, since she is refusing to eat and will die anyway. The old monk cannot accept this, however; it would mean letting the unfaithful gander and the young wench go unpunished. He solves his problem by serving the young goose up to the monks and penning the gander up with his wounded mate! The story is told lightly but sympathetically. The ending is satisfying and appropriate, but handled subtly enough to provide just the right element of surprise.

Most of Griffin's nonfiction works before 1960 deal with three major concerns: censorship, with which he had firsthand experience when *The Devil Rides Outside* was banned in Detroit in 1954; the deeply moving experience of regaining his sight in 1957; and problems of the creative artist. These concerns are reflected in several articles published in *The Nation*, *Southwest Review*, *Reader's Digest*, and other magazines (see bibliography for complete listing). Perhaps more important than these, however, was the monograph Griffin published with Theodore Freedman under the sponsorship of the Anti-Defamation League of B'nai B'rith in 1956, treating the crisis situation resulting from efforts to desegregate the school system in Mansfield, Texas. This monograph

34

objectively reports the difficulties caused by white racists (and condoned by the white majority of Mansfield) and documents the injustices done to Negroes. The events narrated in this monograph supplied the background for a powerful short story, "The Cause," published in *The John Howard Griffin Reader*. The monograph is probably more important, however, as evidence of Griffin's humanitarian concerns and as a foreshadowing of the deepening involvement that was to come four years later with *Black Like Me*.

Griffin's nonfiction works of the Sixties are dominated by articles dealing with racism, mostly echoing the ideas expressed in *Black Like Me*, foreshadowing the culmination of *The Church and the Black Man*, and published in such periodicals as *Saturday Review*, *Southwest Review*, *Christian Century*, *The Texas Observer*, and *Ramparts* (see bibliography for complete listing). Several essays became chapters in books: "Dark Journey," in *The Angry Black*, edited by John A. Williams; "Martin Luther King," in *Thirteen for Christ*, edited by Melville Harcourt; "Dialogue With Father August Thompson," in *Black, White and Gray*, edited by Bradford Daniel; and "Into Mississippi," in *Honey and Wax (The Powers and Pleasures of Narrative)*, edited by Richard Stern.

Griffin had neither intended nor expected to become known primarily as a reporter of and crusader against racism. Looking back on the past decade, he remarked in May, 1969, that his own private bugaboo has been "that a little work that I didn't think was in line with my vocation was the thing that became so overwhelmingly well known. I've always longed for the day when [the problems of racism] would be solved and I could go back"—back to focusing on the humanization of man through creative fiction.

Despite a decade of lectures and the stream of articles on racism culminating in *The Church and the Black Man*, Griffin kept at work in his studio on what he understood to be his original vocation. One of the projects which he managed to complete is his third novel, *Street of the Seven Angels*, currently being prepared for an early-1970 publication by Houghton Mifflin. Griffin has followed his usual practice of structuring the work on musical patterns, this time utilizing the purely classical sonata form in the manner of Mozart. Alternating scenes of great jubilance with scenes of great somberness, the novel echoes Mozart's practice of balancing each phrase with an answering phrase. Like *The Devil Rides Outside*, the new novel contrasts a true sanctity which includes a wholesome earthiness with the false holiness of pharisaical self-righteousness. Unlike the earlier novel, however, *Street of the Seven Angels* is a satire in the Molière vein.

Another book already completed and currently being prepared for publication by Houghton Mifflin is *Scattered Shadows*, an autobiographical volume dealing with Griffin's years of blindness and sight recovery. The first two sections of this book were published in *Ramparts* in January, 1963, and reprinted in *The John Howard Griffin Reader*. These brief excerpts from what will be a lengthy book (600 pages) indicate the nature of what promises to be a deeply moving testament of one man's monumental courage and faith.

Another novel, *Passacaglia*, which Griffin calls "the big one," is now in its fifth draft. Structured on the strict contrapuntal forms of Bach, it is Griffin's most ambitious undertaking to date. Already he has labored on it nearly ten years. It will have to wait a while longer, however, for Griffin has cancelled all public appearances and laid aside his other projects to enter almost total seclusion through mid-1971 to work on the official biography of Thomas Merton, the famed Trappist monk and author who died in 1968.

Once the Merton book is done, Griffin can return not only to *Passacaglia* but also to several other projected books. These include a cultural history of the Tarascan civilization in Mexico; a book-length study of the problems of censorship; a volume on methods

36

of agriculture and livestock production around the world; and a book giving his personal reminiscences about some of the people he has known, illustrated with photographs taken by Griffin himself.

Looking over the body of Griffin's work and taking into account what he can reasonably be expected to produce in the near future, we can see that he clearly represents what Lon Tinkle, book editor of the *Dallas Morning News*, has suggested is a new breed of regional writers: writers who have "come of age" in that they consider themselves not called upon to glorify their region in a chauvinistic sense but who write as full-grown sons of a worldwide intellectual tradition, speaking from and for their region as part of a universal community of man. Although he likes to use regional and local material, Griffin insists that he tries "to destroy all that is contemporary in favor of what is timeless, everything that is regional in favor of what is universal." He seeks to deal with themes that he considers to be of continuing concern to all men everywhere, being careful to create characters who are genuine individuals inhabiting an authentic region.

As the Seventies begin, John Howard Griffin stands in mid-career. After a promising beginning as a novelist, he found himself thrust into the forefront of one of the central struggles of the past decade, the fight against racism. As a new decade begins, even though the problems of racism are far from solved and Griffin will certainly not abandon his zeal for actively seeking to break down the walls of the "cultural prison," it appears that he is once more devoting his main energies to what he considers his central vocation, that of the serious literary artist. The next few years are likely to see several varied works from Griffin's pen and may bring him recognition in literature equal to the acclaim he has already received for his humanitarian endeavors. If this happens, then Maxwell Geismar will not be alone in his praise of the "Texas Balzac."

37

Selected Bibliography

WORKS BY JOHN HOWARD GRIFFIN

BOOKS

The Devil Rides Outside (Fort Worth: Smiths, Inc., 1952; in paperback, New York, Pocket Books, Inc., 1954; also published in England, France, Germany, and Italy).

Nuni (Boston: Houghton Mifflin Company, in association with Smiths, Inc., Dallas, 1956; also published in France and Germany).

Land of the High Sky (Midland, Texas: The First National Bank of Midland, 1959).

Black Like Me (Boston: Houghton Mifflin Company, 1961; in paperback, New York, Signet Books, The New American Library of World Literature, 1962; also published in England, France, Germany, Italy, Norway, Holland, Portugal, Poland, Yugoslavia, Hungary, Czechoslovakia, and Japan).

The John Howard Griffin Reader, ed. Bradford Daniel (Boston: Houghton Mifflin Company, 1968).

The Church and the Black Man (Dayton, Ohio: Pflaum Press, 1969).

MONOGRAPH

A Report of the Crisis Situation Resulting from Efforts to Desegregate the School System, by John Howard Griffin and Theodore Freedman (Field Reports on Desegregation in the South: Mansfield, Texas; [New York, Anti-Defamation League of B'nai B'rith, 1956]).

CHAPTERS IN BOOKS

"Is This What It Means to See?" in *The Spirit of Man*, ed. Whit Burnett (New York: Hawthorn Books, 1958).

"Dark Journey" in *The Angry Black*, ed. John A. Williams (New York: Lancer Books, 1962).

"Martin Luther King" in *Thirteen for Christ*, ed. Melville Harcourt (New York: Sheed and Ward, 1963).

"Dialogue With Father August Thompson" in *Black, White and Gray (21 Points of View on the Race Question),* ed. Bradford Daniel (New York: Sheed and Ward, 1964).

"The Intrinsic Other" in *Building Peace,* ed. Father Georges Dominique Pire, O. P. (Belgium: The Marabou Press, 1966).

"Into Mississippi" in *Honey and Wax (The Powers and Pleasures of Narrative),* ed. Richard Stern (Chicago: University of Chicago Press, 1966).

"Eighteen Covered Wagons" in *A Part of Space: Ten Texas Writers,* ed. Betsy Feagin Colquitt (Ft. Worth: Texas Christian University Press, 1969).

SHORT STORIES

"Miss Henrietta Briggs and Her Metamorphosis" in *Story 3,* ed. Whit Burnett and Hallie Burnett (New York: A. A. Wyn, 1953).

"The Whole World in His Hands" in *New Voices 2: American Writing Today,* ed. Don M. Wolfe (New York: Hendricks House, 1955).

"Sauce for the Gander" in *New World Writing 3* (New York: New American Library, 1953). Also published in *Communicative Reading,* ed. Otis J. Aggertt and Elbert R. Brown (New York: Macmillan, 1956).

"Wooly," *Catholic World,* CLXXXIII (August, 1956), 351-55.

"Chez Durand" in *New World Writing 12* (New York: New American Library, 1957).

ARTICLES

"Withdrawal of the Artist," *The Nation,* CLXXVI (May 2, 1953), 373.

"Prude and the Lewd," *The Nation,* CLXXXI (November 5, 1955), 382-84. Reprinted in Downs, Robert B., ed., *The First Freedom* (Chicago: American Library Association, 1960).

"My Neighbor Reverdy," *Southwest Review,* XLIII (Spring, 1958), 136-42.

"Is This What It Means to See?" (Excerpt from *The Spirit of Man*), *Reader's Digest,* LXXIII (September, 1958), 47-50.

"Journey Into Shame" (Six Installments), *Sepia,* April-September, 1960.

"Journey Into Shame" (Seven part newspaper serial, internationally syndicated; New York: King Features Syndicate, June, 1960).

"The Living Chains of Blackness: Journey Into the Mississippi Night," *Southwest Review,* XLV (Autumn, 1960), 285-92.

"The Men From the Boys," *The Basilian Teacher* (Canada), January, 1961.

The Cultivated Mind—Guardian Genius of Democracy (The University of Dallas, 1962; a specially printed pamphlet studying the contributions of religious institutions to higher education in Texas, 1689-1962).

"Current Trends in Censorship," *Southwest Review*, XLVII (Summer, 1962), 193-200.

"On Either Side of Violence," *Saturday Review*, XLV (October 27, 1962), 38.

"Lillian Smith's *Killers of the Dream*: a Review," *Southwest Review*, XLVII (Winter, 1962), 97-98.

"Scattered Shadows," *Ramparts*, I (January, 1963), 18-34. Two selections from Griffin's autobiography.

"The Shine Boy Has the Dream: Some Afterthoughts on *Black Like Me*," *The Texas Observer*, LV (January 24, 1963), 3-5.

"Dialogue With Father August Thompson," *Ramparts*, II (Christmas Issue, 1963), 24-33.

"Journal of a Trip South," *Ramparts*, II (Christmas Issue, 1963), 35-42.

"The Poulenc Behind the Mask," *Ramparts*, III (October, 1964), 6-8.

"The Tip-Off," *Ramparts*, II (Autumn, 1964).

"Arthur Lourie: A Great Composer Rediscovered," *Ramparts*, III (January, 1965), 32-34.

"A Visit to Huy," *Ramparts*, IV (August, 1965), 27-30.

"Maritain Charts a Course Through Change," *National Catholic Reporter*, November 9, 1966.

WORKS ABOUT JOHN HOWARD GRIFFIN

Bartlett, Bertrice, and Manske, Dwain, "An Interview with John Howard Griffin," *The Texas Observer*, LII (July 1, 1960), 6.

Blakey, G. Robert, "Obscenity and the Supreme Court," *America*, CXIII (August 13, 1966), 152-56.

Cargas, Harry J., "Who Is John Howard Griffin?" *St. Louis Review*, May 28, 1965.

Daniel, Bradford, "Why They Can't Wait: An Interview With a White Negro," *The Progressive*, XXVIII (July, 1964), 15-19.

———, "The Noble Vision of Father Pire," *Ramparts*, IV (August, 1965), 20-26. Discussion of Griffin's association with Father Georges Dominique Pire, O. P., and the University of Peace, Huy, Belgium.

41

Fixx, J. F., "The South's Other War," *Saturday Review,* XLV (April 14, 1962), 22-23+.

Geismar, Maxwell, "John Howard Griffin: The Devil in Texas," *American Moderns* (New York: Hill and Wang, 1958), pp. 251-65.

Library Journal, LXXVII (October 15, 1952), 1802. Biographical sketch.

Lomax, Louis E., "It's Like This," *Saturday Review,* XLIV (December 9, 1961), 53-54.

McDonnell, Thomas P., "John Howard Griffin: An Interview," *Ramparts,* I (January, 1963), 6-16.

McNamara, Eugene, "Prospects of a Catholic Novel," *America,* XCVII (August 17, 1957), 506.

————, "The Post-Modern American Novel," *Queen's Quarterly,* LXIX (Summer, 1962), 265-75.

Montgomery, Ruth, "John Howard Griffin: A Biographical Study," *Wilson Library Bulletin,* XXXVII (May, 1963), 802.

Rank, H., "Rhetorical Effectiveness of *Black Like Me,*" *English Journal,* LVII (September, 1968), 813-17.

Sussman, Irving, and Cornelia, *How to Read a Dirty Book* (Chicago: Franciscan Herald Press, 1966).

DATE DUE